JUST SAY THE WORD

ENDORSEMENTS

"Every husband needs help and encouragement in praying with his wife...Sam provides both in Just Say The Word. I've done what he recommends and it works! Try this for 30 days and your marriage will never be the same!"

Dr. Dennis Rainey

Host, FamilyLife Today

"Sam Ingrassia is on to something. For years I struggled when it came to praying with my wife. Why? Because she is light years ahead of me when it comes to getting in touch with God. And I'm a pastor! It seems that we men need help, and we need a plan. Well, here it is. Just Say the Word is a biblical and simple way for a husband and wife to pray together. Praying through the Scriptures, or "expository praying," as Sam calls it, works. If you have tried and failed to keep a consistent prayer life with the love of your life, then this book is for you! My wife JoAnn and I hit our knees first thing in the morning and pray through the Bible together. We're in the book of Hebrews right now, and our prayer time has never been better as a couple. Thank you, Sam! God's hand is on this book. Pastors, this book will help marriages in your church. Challenge your men to read Just Say the Word."

Tom Doyle

Author of *Dreams and Visions: Is Jesus Awakening the Muslim World?*

Vice-President of e3 Partners Ministry

Do you pray with your wife?' Sam's challenge to me hit me square in the heart because I wasn't doing it. I realized that I cannot be the husband, the father, the man of God I desire to be if I don't take care of and nurture the most important gift that God gave me — my wife. Just Say the Word *lays out a road map for any man to follow the direction of the Holy Spirit and draw closer with his spouse through prayer. I encourage all husbands to take the first step and 'Just Say the Word' with their wives.*

Chad Hennings
Founder, Wingmen Ministries and
Three-time Super Bowl Champion

Have you found it difficult—maybe impossible—to lead your home spiritually? For any man who answers "yes" to this question, Sam Ingrassia has great news! In a short read, Just Say the Word *describes a simple practice you can start today, one that will transform your marriage and your life. Get it!*

Nate Larkin
Author of *Samson and the Pirate Monks:*
Calling Men to Authentic Brotherhood
Founder of the Samson Society

Of course, I should pray with my wife. I know that! What I don't know is how to do it. This is the real problem. Don't just tell me what to do. Help me find a way to do it.

Sam Ingrassia does just that in his deeply personal and disarmingly transparent book. The problem is universal, and the solution is for every man who wants to be the spiritual leader in his home. Man, when you pray with her you plumb the depths of God's promises covering that ancient and most precious of relationships. One flesh, He said, and meant it. Your marriage is in for a shot in the arm.

Jim and Kaye Johns
Authors of *Higher Ground, Deeper Truth*
and *Prayers for the Moment*
Founders, PrayerPower Ministries

JUST SAY
THE WORD

JUST SAY
THE WORD

a simple way
to increase your
passion for God
and your wife

Sam Ingrassia

Published by PrayerPower Publishing
P.O. Box 801368
Dallas, TX 75380-1368

Published in association with New Vantage Partners—Franklin, TN
info@NewVantagePartners.net

Design and typesetting by Paul Gant Art & Design – Franklin, TN

Prayer P🔥wer

P U B L I S H I N G
www.prayerpowerministries.org

ISBN: 978-0-9853038-1-5

Third printing

Printed in the United States of America

DEDICATION
To my wife, Vicki

I cannot even remotely imagine life without you. I deeply respect your walk with God and how He uniquely uses you to touch so many lives. This book was born really from your heart as much as from my own. I love you dearly.

CONTENTS

BIBLICAL AND SIMPLE

An epidemic afflicts our generation! Many—dare I say most—Christian men live with the burden lurking in their hearts and minds that they are failing to provide spiritual leadership for their wives. This is even true among godly Christian men who are helping others pursue God. We are not initiating regular and intentional spiritual connection with our wives. Sure, we share spiritual life from time to time, but not on a regular and intentional basis. What am I talking about? Simply this: *Praying together.*

Be honest. Beyond dinner prayers, bedtime prayers with children or praying at church, in a typical week, how often do you and your wife pray together? Just the two of you?

A candid answer is likely not a comfortable one. I know that because of the answers from my own life. I have also posed this question, eyeball to eyeball, with a host of Christian brothers. And I know how their answers fare.

I know you don't need any additional guilt today. Nor do I desire to load you further. It is important to recognize how we have failed because the admission can give way to the repentance of mind and heart, which can open us to viable and lasting changes. But mourning the past, or even the present, will not provide lasting motivation and change.

We need to see something ahead. And that something is an opportunity. *I tell you: the opportunity is ripe for us to step into our role and see*

God show up in very real ways.

My hope is to share a model and call you to a challenge, which is not only **biblical**, but also **simple** to embrace. It will lead you and your wife to a fresh dimension in your spiritual walk together. You will be bolstered in the storms of life. You will be equipped to provide and protect your marriage and family with confidence. It will impact your children and grandchildren. In fact, it will touch every dimension of your life.

God has brought this matter to the forefront of attention in my own life. And I thank Him for doing so. My wife thanks Him for it as well! I want to share my story so that with me you can welcome your role with hope and resolve.

CHAPTER 1

MY GREAT AWAKENING

When that nagging alarm clock rings in the morning you have options. Some people immediately jump out of bed. Some people use the "snooze" button! Hitting "snooze" through a fog of sleepiness is saying, "Later . . . Not yet . . . I don't want to get up quite yet . . . I need more time to sleep!"

One of my daughters is a "3-snooze" person. She just can't wake up abruptly. So she strategically plans ahead to hit the snooze button three times. This way she can gradually awaken to face her day.

God, too, has an alarm clock. However, His alarm rings, not to arouse Him, but us. It rings to awaken us to attend to different dimensions of our lives. When His alarm rings, we have options. One is that we can answer the alarm, get up, and address the issue at hand. Another is to "hit the snooze button." Essentially we are saying, "Later, God! I need a little more time. Then I will get to it."

I believe God's alarm is ringing today in the lives of many Christian husbands. Maybe it has been ringing for a long time. And many of us have been hitting the snooze button . . . for a long time.

The Miraculous Return of Our Prodigal Daughter

The day after Easter in March 2008 our family saw a phenomenal miracle of God! Our first daughter Christina had wandered from the Lord into the "broad way leading to destruction." This wayward journey encompassed a substantial portion of her late teens, through college, and stretching into her young adult years.

My wife Vicki and I sought to raise our three daughters the best we knew how and to pour Christ into them. We went to church regularly. In fact, I was an associate pastor of the church! They went to Sunday school, youth groups, and summer camps—the whole nine yards.

Some of you know exactly what I am talking about. Perhaps you have done some "broad way" time in your own life! Or maybe you are suffering right now from the antics of a wayward child. You've done all you know to do as a Christian parent. You seek to be a sufficient role model in your home as a believer in Jesus Christ.

STILL, the reality is that your kids and grandkids ultimately need to "own their own faith." And just as it was with us, they learn the most about really owning their faith in the Lord from encountering troubles. And it appears that some people need to "taste blood, sweat and tears" to learn to own their faith. The broad way is the perfect place to encounter "blood, sweat and tears." For some complexity of reasons, Christina ended up in a really bad place in her life. She never renounced Jesus Christ. But she was really far from Him.

(We have had the privilege of sharing our story in several churches. The audio of our testimony, "Parenting Wayward Children," is available at www.2mites.org. If you know somebody who has teenage or adult children who are "out there," you might want to refer them to this talk. We are happy to know the Lord has used our story to bring hope to many suffering parents.)

One wonderful day, Christina dramatically returned to the Lord in a profound repentance. God broke into the center place of her attention. He moved powerfully in her heart. She truly surrendered to Him and embarked upon what has become a complete transformation of her life. Now she is seriously seeking to walk with God.

A friend of mine pointed out that, "When these kids go out there far from God and then He brings them back, they don't come back normal, they come back warriors!" That exactly describes what God has done for Christina, and we are deeply grateful to God for His marvelous miracle of grace in our family.

Let me declare to you the wondrous truth, which I told Christina the night she came home. God can "restore the years the locusts have eaten" (Joel 2:25). We praise Him for this grace!

"You Have Failed Me"

A fair label you could post across every marriage would be "Under Construction." The goal of maintaining unity in marriage is a moving target, largely because the stages of life continuously face us with fresh challenges like:

- Newlywed adjustments;
- Caring for babies and young children (24/7!);
- Or perhaps facing struggles of infertility;

- Struggling to find balance in raising teenagers;
- College years and the attendant costs;
- Ups and downs of aging and health;
- Uncertainty in financial conditions;
- Instability with employment during insecure economic times;
- Geographic moves;
- Handling trials, troubles, and temptations;
- Attending to aging and ailing parents.

On and on . . . . Life is real, difficult, and challenging!

Vicki and I have been together in life for almost four decades, and sometimes it feels as if I have no idea where all those years have gone. We came to personal faith in Jesus Christ at the same time during our college days. Since then, we have journeyed the Christian life together. We desire and seek to have a Christ-centered marriage. Yet the "under construction" aspect of marriage means it is an on-going and on-*growing* relationship-in-progress.

And so, Vicki and I ran into a bit of rough patch. A number of issues bubbled around, churning up stress and tension. When all of that ripples over into multiple areas of life, things can get pretty confusing.

I enjoy fishing and, like most fishermen, I suppose, have discovered that sometimes a poor cast will "backlash" and create a bird's nest of tangled fishing line. If that happens, you are through fishing for a while! Untangling the wadded up mass of line can be a time-consuming chore—and very frustrating. So one afternoon, Vicki and I realized our line had backlashed. We sat in our living room and attempted to work our way through this difficult season. We were trying to figure out "just what is going on?"

As we talked, something emerged from Vicki's heart, which she realized was a key part of what was unsettling for her. "You know what, Sam?" she told me, "Part of what is going on here is that . . . you have failed me."

The words were far from normal for my wife to say! She got my attention. "You have failed me" was the last thing I wanted to hear from the woman I have loved for more than forty years.

Her words did not arise from long-standing bitterness but from a realization that finally came to light for her. She went on to say, "You failed me, because during Christina's long journey in the broad way, you did not pray with me to consistently fight for her soul over those years. I largely felt like I had to do it on my own."

This does not mean we never prayed together for our daughter. But it did mean that I had not provided the spiritual leadership and initiative to consistently pray with Vicki for our wayward daughter. I had neglected to intentionally and regularly lead us together with the weapon of prayer to fight for our daughter's soul. Vicki was dead right!

At the core of the rough patch was the painful reality that our girls were facing a number of serious issues in their lives. Vicki was burdened that, as their parents, she and I needed to be praying together about those matters. Reflecting upon my lack of spiritual leadership in prayer, she continued, "I am emotionally tired and worn out. I just cannot do this alone again."

But even that wasn't all. "Sam," she pleaded, "beyond praying for our daughters, the fact is *I need to connect with you spiritually.*"

I knew immediately she was right. We needed to be sharing spiritual life together. Sure, to a degree we were. But I would have to describe our spiritual lives as haphazardly "touching together spiritually." We sort of "bumped along" in occasional spiritual connectedness. We would go to church regularly, pray at meals, talk about a sermon we heard, share spiritual insights, and so on. But it definitely lacked intentionality and regular initiative from me. The missing piece was the consistent, intentional connection of praying together.

"For the Revelation Awaits an Appointed Time!"

Habakkuk was an Old Testament prophet who complained a lot to God. Habakkuk thought God needed to show up and handle all the foolishness and sin which was evident among His people. So God shocked Habakkuk by announcing that He was preparing the Babylonians to bring a judgment upon His people. In Habakkuk 2:3 God explained, "For the revelation awaits an appointed time; it speaks of the end and will not prove false. Though it linger, wait for it; it will certainly come and will not delay" (NIV).

Did you catch that line: "for the revelation awaits an appointed time"?

Some months before my showdown with Vicki, that concept had been impressed upon me from this verse. It is about the sovereignty of God. God reveals in His timing.

When the light goes on (or the alarm goes off!) in our lives, usually it is not because we learn new *information*. Often we already have the information, and what we need is the *revelation*. In the mystery of God, it is also about His "appointed time."

This is a mystery to me. Sometimes I think God's timing is pretty bad, don't you? But we are not God. Certainly only God always understands the reason for His timing. Sometimes we have a glimpse of understanding, but frequently we are in the dark. It is an evident call for us to trust Him.

Guilty!

That afternoon with Vicki, I had the revelation! As all of this came tumbling out of my wife's heart, I literally lifted up my hands, as if being arrested, and said, "Guilty . . . guilty as charged!" The conviction of God fell heavy upon me. The alarm was ringing with more force and volume than ever before, and I couldn't hit the snooze button any longer. I was really broken. I felt terrible. I confessed to Vicki, "It hardly seems sufficient to cover the scope of what we are talking about here, but I want to tell you I am sorry. With all my heart, I am so sorry!"

"It Is Not Going to Happen Again"

It is a wonderful thing to realize the attendant grace of God. As the revelation of conviction and repentance fell upon me, simultaneously a firm resolve gripped my heart. I said, "You know what, Vicki? By the grace of God, this is *not* going to happen again. I *promise*. It is *not* going to happen again!" I sensed my words were at the level of the vows I had given her at the wedding altar.

I continued, "The best we can, within the reasonable limitations and realities of life, we are going to pray together. I know life is very busy, unpredictable, a moving target, but daily prayer together will be the goal. And I am going to take the lead in initiating. I vow to be *intentional*."

"The Bible Will Be Our Template!"

Suddenly, I even knew how we were going to make this work.

I told Vicki, "Here is how we are going to do it. We are going to pray the Bible! We will let the Bible literally be the guide for our prayers. The Bible will be our template. We are going to intentionally follow God's Word in our prayers—Scripture praying.

"We will read a paragraph of the Bible together — see how the Holy Spirit might speak to our hearts— and then we will let the text of the Bible be the guide for what we will pray back to God.

"We will run on the tracks of the Scriptures to give us the ideas and content for our prayers. Then we will pray about a few of the other things that are immediately at hand in our lives, family, and ministry—and that is it. We will keep it short, and then we will be on our way."

Since it is one my favorite books of the Bible, I suggested we start with the book of Hebrews. And you know what? It was just awesome!

Expository Praying

Think about it! What could be better than praying the Word of God itself? The will of God, the truths, principles, prayers, praises, values, and doctrines of God.

Perhaps you have heard of "expository preaching." An expository preacher preaches through the Bible, verse-by-verse, paragraph-by-paragraph. He allows God's Word to bring forth the message for God's people. The Bible becomes the guide to provide the content, ideas, concepts, and exhortations of his preaching and teaching. This approach allows the message to emerge from the Word of God.

So let's call our approach "Expository Praying." We can follow the Bible with our prayers. God's Word will be the guide to show us the topics, ideas, praises, and requests. In doing so, we allow God to show us what to pray about. We "call out" God's Word in our prayers. The Bible gives us the tracks to follow, and in this way, we can be sure our prayers are on track.

Not Spiritual Enough

I am neither creative enough nor spiritual enough to pray with the same person on a daily or very regular basis and sweep the heavens with all kinds of "thee's," "thou's," spiritual insights, and wonderful intercessions. Praying every time about basically the same things in the same way, I would be boring and/or bored in short order.

But by following the Word of God and by letting the Bible literally be the text of our prayers, then the Bible will take care of keeping our prayers fresh.

It will enable us to be as creative and comprehensive as the Bible itself! We will be praying "on target"—the Word and will of God over our lives, family and ministry—in an ever fresh and empowered manner.

A Terrifying Thing Happened

I came from a religious background that taught and modeled for me that prayers consisted of reciting to God memorized words which have been passed down through the centuries. I vividly recall mindlessly reciting such prayers on many occasions. That is all I knew to do.

Then I trusted in Jesus Christ as my Savior during my college days and started my journey with the Lord. I remember attending the first Bible study of my life. When it came time to pray, the leader launched into spontaneously talking out loud to God! He seemed know what to say.

Then a terrifying thing happened. Other people

in the group, taking turns one-by-one, also started to "talk out loud to God." They had creative words in prayers right off the top of their heads! I found myself thinking with my heart pounding, "Oh, no, what if they expect me to do this, too?" But thankfully that did not happen.

Quickly I recognized that, as a Christian, I needed somehow to learn to do this. I needed to be ready, on the spot, at any time, to launch into a spontaneous and extemporaneous (and eloquent, I might add) prayer to God. I thought I had to impress everyone praying with me, and especially to remember that God is listening!

Perhaps these words and emotions from my past constitute your present situation. Maybe you and/or your wife are hesitant to pray out loud. If so, that is just fine. Honestly, it's all the more reason for suggesting that the Bible is the perfect guide to help you find the words to say in front of the Lord and each another. I promise: this will work for you.

On the other hand, maybe you are completely comfortable voicing extemporaneous prayers. Perhaps you have been doing it for years.

Even so, I would suggest that following the Bible in Expository Praying will bring a freshness and vitality to prayers with your wife. In fact, your prayer time may become more alive than ever.

NOT THE ONLY ONE

Vicki and I started into this model of praying through books of the Bible and had a wonderful time together. We began to see some great things happen. We were intentionally connecting together spiritually more regularly than ever before. God was answering some special prayers. We were observing and learning some helpful truths from God's Word.

Yet, after we were praying together for a season, I began to sense a prompting from the Lord. God wanted me to use my personal failure in praying with my wife as a platform to call other Christian men out on this same issue.

So I started to do just that. Gradually, as God seemed to prompt my heart, I would grab lunch with one of my friends and share my story. Then I would ask him the "big question"—the one about how he was doing with his wife in the area of praying together.

Godly Men Struggling

I serve full time in missions with e3 Partners Ministry, a missions group which mobilizes teams of North Americans in a short-term missions model. Our approach is to preach the Gospel to help churches and pastors around the world strengthen and start new churches. Given my calling and career, most of the men in my immediate circle of contact are pastors, elders, missionaries, Christian leaders, and businessmen who are strong Christians.

Therefore, in most instances, I have been sharing this story and challenge with men who would be recognized as Christian leaders. They are godly men, intending to guide and influence others for Jesus Christ and for the growth of His Church and the advancement of His Kingdom.

I sit across the table from them and share my story. Then I turn the issue toward them, saying, "I want to ask you a personal question. You are my friend, but you can lie to me or tell me the truth. You can decide [they usually chuckle], but here is the question: Apart from prayers at meals, praying to put children to bed, or praying at church or a meeting, how often do you and your wife pray together . . . just the two of you?"

What I suspected has proven true. Most every Christian man is living with some level of burden that he is not providing adequate spiritual leadership at home with his wife—particularly evident by the lack of prayer alone together as husband and wife. When I ask the "big question," I find that, just like me, they are bumping along, connecting spiritually in only a haphazard way. Invariably they say something like, "Sam, I am exactly like you described it!"

Pay attention . . . this is important! I am not interested in heaping more guilt on you. If you are reading a book like this, you obviously desire to be a spiritual leader for your wife and family. But the struggle simply boils down to one core issue: **we men simply do not know what to do!** We are trying to guide our families for Jesus Christ. We are seeking to "do the right things." But we somehow know and feel there is a linchpin missing.

You can step forward confidently and with growing success. I am excited to give you hope! You can enjoy increasing "wins" as a spiritual leader with your wife and family. This model is clearly biblical and do-able.

Intimidated

As I talk to men about their marriages, I notice a frequent pattern. It appears that most of us assess our wives as "ahead of us" in having a heart for God and pursuing Him. When push comes to shove, we would say our wives are "more spiritual than I am." So we wonder, "What am I supposed to do to lead *her spiritually*? I mean, what do you want me to do with her?"

A motivated guy might go to a Christian bookstore and find some type of devotional booklet with questions to answer with his wife: "OK, dear, let's read this booklet, some Bible verses, and try to answer these questions. OK, question #1, what does the Greek word *metanoia* mean?"

Such resources can be good for a season, but they sometimes feel "canned" and possibly not so helpful or practical. Over the long haul, this approach seems to fade away to nothing. I remember one friend telling me, "it was not comfortable, and it is hard to keep doing something that is not comfortable—so our time together felt stilted and stale. So we ended up just quitting and doing nothing again."

You Do Not Need to "Disciple Your Wife"

I have a thought for you to ponder, one you might find freeing. I did! Your wife does not need you to disciple her—at least in the sense that she does not need you to impart "spiritual information" to her. Yet she does desire and need you to lead her spiritually.

Your wife does not desire to "sit at your feet" so you can bless her with an unending string of spiritual pearls of wisdom and insight (as if we had such a string of pearls to offer). Rather, she wants to "sit at your side" and face life with a true spiritual perspective together. Remember that in Genesis this whole thing started when God fashioned woman out of a rib from man's side. Our wives are not intended to be "under us," or "over us," but "beside us." That is Christian marriage.

Leading your wife spiritually is not about imparting information. It is about walking in relationship—a relationship of three: husband, wife, and God. It is not about *how much you know* to impart to her. It is about *who you are* as her partner in life and your commitment to live in yoke together with her—and with Jesus Christ.

We have an ill-informed view of discipleship. We tend toward thinking about discipleship as information-centric. That's a big mistake! Discipleship is relationship-centric. Discipleship is walking side-by-side with someone in the realities of life. This includes the mountaintop blessings, the curses of the deep, dark valleys, and everything in between. Leading your wife spiritually is just that—

walking side-by-side with her through the realities of life. You don't lag behind her in the journey or run ahead of her. Leading in marriage is not done from "out front." It is done from her side.

Just Say the Word will equip you as never before to step into your role, confidently and effectively, by her side.

Answers of Abdication

So I ask my friends, "How often do you and your wife pray together—just the two of you?"

What kind of answers do you think I am hearing?

Will you pause right here a moment and give your answer?

Virtually every time the responses are in the extreme. Answers like:

- Never
- Rarely
- Maybe 3 times a year
- Hardly ever
- Occasionally
- When it is needed—problems or crises, of course
- Not enough
- And I love this one: "When she asks me to!"

These men are being brutally honest with me (I imagine the honesty is encouraged since I have just spilled the guts of my own failure). In any case, it is clear that these answers are consistently at the far end of the spectrum, down in the range of "abdication."

It might not be too strong a description to say these answers are tragic. In saying this, remember I am speaking from my own platform of having largely failed and abdicated my own responsibility for not merely years, but for several *decades*!

My friends often admit, "Sam, we are now where you have been. We go to church, we pray at meals in our home and maybe even in a restaurant, we seek to be a spiritual family. I want to follow God, and my passion is that my family will follow the Lord. But what you are talking about in a regular, intentional prayer time with my wife—I am not doing it either."

We typically don't get very far into this discussion before the men feel fairly convicted and guilty—just as I did. Some have had tears in their eyes, but over and over I have been amazed as they testify to the perfect timing of this challenge for their lives and marriages.

I then call them to consider a commitment and accountability together with me. "Let's work together to improve our spiritual leadership with our wives. Let's move toward more intentional spiritual connection by using the Bible as the guiding tracks for our prayers."

What Would She Say?

At some point in my meeting with the men I encourage to take this challenge, I ask, "Suppose your wife were sitting here right now. If we told her you have made a decision to step into this commitment to meet together with her on a more intentional and regular basis—to read some of the Bible and pray together, using the Bible text as a guide to pray over your family and some immediate needs—what would she say?"

What kind of answers do you suppose I hear to that question? Again they are extreme. But this time they are at the other end of the spectrum:

- She would be overwhelmed!
- She would say I have been waiting for this for 14 years!
- She would fall out of the chair!
- She would say I have been praying for this!
- She would start crying!
- She would say, "Hallelujah!"
- She would say, "Yes, when do we start?"

These answers from Christian husbands reveal several terribly important things we already know. We already know that:

1. Our wives genuinely long for our spiritual leadership which can be expressed through praying with them.

2. They will be willing and ready to step into more intentional prayer with us, if we resolve to initiate.

3. God's alarm has been ringing in this area of our lives, and we have been hitting the snooze button—some of us for a long time.

4. We need to do a better job of connecting emotionally and spiritually with our wives.

How About You?

I cannot sit across a lunch table from you, but I'm asking you to think about two things:

1. Honestly assess where you are in your life and marriage with this issue of intentionally and regularly praying with your wife. Simply put: how often do you and your wife pray together— just the two of you?

2. Would you be willing to step toward praying with your wife in a more intentional and regular way? I am proposing a model that will help you do exactly that. We are talking about Intentional Spiritual Intimacy.

INTENTIONAL
SPIRITUAL INTIMACY

Think with me about God's description of marriage in Genesis 2:24-25 using the words "one flesh":

> For this cause a man shall leave his
> father and his mother, and shall cleave
> to his wife; and they shall become one
> flesh. And the man and his wife were
> both naked and not ashamed. (NASB)

An in-depth look at this passage is beyond the scope and purpose of this book, but we need to recognize God's basic description of marriage. The key ideas are not difficult to identify:

- Leave;
- Cleave;
- One flesh;
- Naked and not ashamed.

The man is to leave his family of origin, to join together with his wife as "one flesh." The relationship is intimate in every dimension. There is no shame.

You and your wife are "one flesh" before God. This is not simply a metaphor, idea, or illustration. This is a spiritual, mystical reality before God. Yes, God sees the Christian husband and wife, each as an individual child before Him. But in the union of marriage, you and your wife are *one*. One plus one...

equals one. This is a critical reality to grasp. We know it, but do we really understand it?

Union = Life

God has designed our bodies so that when a husband and wife come together in sexual intimacy, life is created. Our joining each other has life-creating, life-giving power. Physical union yields physical life.

As a result of physical intimacy, children are conceived and birthed. From physical union with my wife, God has chosen to create through us three daughters who are eternal beings. If you pause to really think about it, it is *amazing*!

In this one-flesh connection, God has ordained creative power. He told Adam and Eve to go forth, multiply, and fill the earth. This is the one command from God men are delighted to obey. "Oh, yes, God. Right away, Lord!"

The same life-generating dynamic is true with spiritual intimacy. *Spiritual union yields spiritual life.* When you come together with your wife spiritually, in prayer, with the living Word of God, God desires to conceive and birth life—His Life! He can bring to life:

- Insights
- Ideas
- Love
- Joy
- Peace
- Answered prayers

◗ Emotional health
◗ Transparency and honesty
◗ Spiritual growth
◗ Unity
◗ And much more.

Your spiritual and emotional connection with your wife can be very powerful. In fact, this may be difficult for you to imagine, but your prayers with your wife are more vital and effective than the prayers of anyone else. It doesn't matter if she has a best girlfriend who is her prayer partner or if a spiritual pastor were to pray with her every day. Because you are in one-flesh union, your prayers with your wife are more important than the prayers of any other person.

Umbrella of Spiritual Union

Imagine a spiritual umbrella covering over your marriage, family, life and ministry. The life-giving power of God is showing up to cover your lives. You are praying the Word of God, the will of God, the values, truths, principles, blessings, and intercessions from the Bible. Your spiritual connection in marriage will pour life into your lives. What an exciting opportunity!

Your wife needs this connection. Your children need this connection. Your grandchildren need this connection. You need this connection. The spiritual union of your marriage will cover your lives and your whole family.

The Marriage Triangle

You likely have heard marriage illustrated as a triangle. God is at the top of the triangle. Husband and wife are at each of the bottom corners. As each of you draws near to God, moving up the sides of the triangle, you will be moving closer to one another. The intention is to illustrate the benefits of having God at the center of your marriage relationship.

Just saying the Word with your wife helps this triangle dynamic spring to life. This prayer journey is the triangle lived out in a practical and real manner.

Imagine this marriage triangle as an electrical circuit. A complete circuit is required for the power to flow. A short circuit happens when the wires are not connecting properly. You wiggle the wires to find only short surges of power coming through. This is like our marriages when we are bumping along, haphazardly connecting spiritually. Praying together completes the marriage triangle circuit. Connecting in your one-flesh spiritual union by praying the Bible together can activate the power, presence, and perspectives of God over your marriage, lives, children, family, ministry, and career.

This is not a "gimmick" for manipulating God to do what we want Him to do. It is a call to practically enter deeper into God's sacred design for the union of marriage. We can connect more intentionally as we use the Bible as our guide to pray together. We can simply allow God to show us what to pray about.

Yoke and Vine

Two illustrations from the teaching of Jesus are centered on the important concept of connectedness. They are the Yoke and the Vine.

In Matthew 11:28-30, Jesus calls us to take His yoke that we might learn from Him:

> Come to me all you who are weary and
> burdened, and I will give you rest. Take
> my yoke upon you and learn from me,
> for I am gentle and humble in heart, and
> you will find rest for your souls. For my
> yoke is easy and my burden is light.

In John 15:4-5, Jesus reveals the necessity of the branch remaining in connection with the vine to yield fruit:

> Remain in me, and I will remain in you.
> No branch can bear fruit by itself; it
> must remain in the vine. Neither can you
> bear fruit unless you remain in me. I am
> the vine; you are the branches. If a man
> remains in me and I in him, he will bear
> much fruit; apart from me you can do
> nothing.

Although unpacking the rich teachings in these verses is beyond the scope of this book, with these two illustrations, Jesus is calling us to connect with God. This is the only path to rest and fruitfulness. God exists as a Trinity (or tri-unity), and His perfect desire for union and connectedness is reflected in the creation of marriage as a one-flesh relationship.

Praying together as husband and wife enhances our union with God. We also connect more deeply with one another in this spiritual union. Praying together as husband and wife is also a practical way to take the "yoke of Jesus" and to "remain connected to the vine." We will learn together from the gentle, humble heart of Jesus Christ and become increasingly fruitful for our joy and His glory.

Intentional Spiritual Intimacy

We are talking here about Intentional Spiritual Intimacy in marriage. As a husband, you can become more intentional, rather than haphazard, in your spiritual leadership. You can pursue more regular times to pray with your wife if you are equipped with an approach that is comfortable and helpful. Using the Bible as a prayer guide is the do-able model to help us.

Living with Deprivation

You likely expect your wife to be available to you for a diet of physical intimacy which works in your marriage. This dimension of connection in marriage is important to holistic marital health. Certainly this is vital to you as a man and husband. Typically men more regularly desire and need sexual intimacy. We know it. Our wives know it.

Yet, we also know she has spiritual and emotional needs, and we might not be making ourselves available to her! Over time, we have taught our wives to learn to live deprived. How would we fare, if our wives were not available for our physical needs? Yet we have abdicated our responsibility, depriving her of spiritual intimacy.

Sometimes we think ourselves disqualified from spiritual intimacy with our wives because of the issues, sins, and shortcomings in our lives. But I dare say we rarely, if ever, disqualify ourselves from physical intimacy because of our issues! When is the last time you said, "Honey, let's not have sex because I have some struggles in my life"? It seems we find a way to put things aside when it comes to sexual intimacy. Hmmm. What is that about?

In part of that fateful conversation I had with my wife, she said to me, "Honey, if we had sexual intimacy as often as we prayed together, you would be pretty disappointed." Wow, that's not pulling any punches! You are welcome to laugh, but how true is this in your marriage?

The bottom line is this: *If you are making time in your marriage for physical intimacy, you need to be making time for spiritual intimacy.* Tension over physical intimacy in marriage is a common issue. I am not minimizing this complicated issue at all. And I sincerely do not intend this as a tool of manipulation. However, if we were to connect more consistently with our wives spiritually and emotionally, the benefits and blessings are likely to show up in our physical intimacy as well. If we love our wives expressed as in time spent reading and praying through the Bible together, they will likely desire to give themselves to us more fully.

Answer the Alarm

Has the alarm been ringing in your life? Have you been hitting the snooze button for too long?

To whatever extent this challenge applies to you, I am asking you to quit abdicating. There is really no credible excuse for our failure as Christian men, husbands, and leaders. Even among godly men who are helping other people pursue God, we are not "hitting on all eight" at home. And this abdication appears to be epidemic!

The challenge is not only about regretting how we have failed in the past. It is about looking to future opportunity. We can step toward a vital connection with our wives that will yield abundant spiritual, emotional, and relational fruit.

Remember these realities:

- Physical one-flesh intimacy creates physical life.
- Spiritual one-flesh intimacy creates spiritual life.

THE APPROACH

When sighting in a rifle, you typically place a stationary target at 100 or 200 yards. You settle the crosshairs of your scope as steady as you can, perfectly on the bull's-eye. Test firings must be consistent. Depending upon placement of the shots, you adjust the scope to shift your shots precisely to the center of the target. Sounds easy, right?

Now imagine sighting in your rifle if the target were not stationary but moving around while you're sighting it in. Difficult for sure, right? But doesn't that sound a little like the way we live our lives? Life itself is a moving target!

We need a supernatural scope to consistently hit the bull's-eye of life. This is exactly why I am suggesting we not only read the Bible but also learn to pray the Bible. By recommending the Word of God as a literal guide for our prayers, I am not suggesting we are using it as a "magic book" or as method for "manipulating God." Not at all!

Often we hardly know what or how to pray because the target of life is moving quickly and seemingly at random. As we pray the Word of God, though, the Holy Spirit guides us. He will help us hit not only the target but even the bull's-eye from time to time.

Your First Step

The first step you must take is to tell your wife of the "revelation" you have received. Tell her of your new commitment by God's grace. It could be that you owe your wife an apology. A true apology does not just express sorrow. You also need to ask for her forgiveness. And understand that forgiveness is given once repentance is demonstrated. In other words, repentance lived out over reasonable time opens the door to reconciliation and forgiveness. She needs to see that your apology has substance. Behavior change over time puts skin on apology.

My wife did not mention it, but I am certain there was some skepticism in a corner of her heart. Imagine that your wife has her arms crossed and is saying, "OK, we will see what happens over time." You and I need to live out our resolve.

One friend shared with me that he told his wife of his resolve, and he apologized for his previous lack of spiritual leadership. His wife said, "You have no idea how much your apology means to me!" His acknowledgment and confession touched her heart more than he could have anticipated.

Practical, *Do-able* Steps:

1. Decide.
Decide on a book of the Bible to get started. Perhaps you can decide together. Do either of you have a favorite book? Often I have recommended Philippians as a good starting point. Another good place is the Psalms. The Psalms is a book of songs, so the words of the Psalms provide a perfect guide for us to pray. We can voice in our prayers the same words David voiced to the Lord!

2. Read.

Read out loud what seems to be a reasonable selection of verses. Don't try to bite off too much. I recommend proceeding slowly. You can both participate in reading if you like. Approach it in whatever fashion is most comfortable for your marriage.

3. Observations.

We usually sit quietly for a minute or two. We are asking the Holy Spirit to speak to our hearts so we can make a few observations from the text. I often say something like, "Honey, what do you see? Are there any key words or phrases that jump out at you? Any key ideas or concepts? Any special thoughts, insights or applications? What do you think is the main idea or topic in these verses?" I like to allow my wife to speak first, if possible. This allows me to hear her heart and understand how God speaks to her. You could very easily find yourselves starting to discuss many things, but—warning —you are not here to teach the Bible to your wife. This is not a teaching time; it is a season of prayer.

4. Pray together.

You are on "holy ground" as you come together in one-flesh spiritual intimacy with your wife. The Holy Spirit will bring encouragement to both you and your wife.

▶ *Focus on key words and topics from the text.* Remember this approach is Expository Praying. Pray using the literal words from the verses in a spirit of prayer. We can follow the Bible with our prayers. God's Word is the guide to show us the content, topics, ideas, praises, and requests. Allow God to show you and your wife what to pray. The Bible will give you the tracks to follow.

For example, in Philippians 4:10-13, Paul talks about being content. So from this text, we prayed about the issue of contentment in our lives and in the lives of our daughters. Someone might be struggling in his or her place of employment, and you can pray that the person will discover contentment in having gainful employment during a difficult economy.

▶ *Each of you can participate.* Take turns praying out loud. Each person prays a short time. Whatever the case, proceed as is comfortable for your marriage. However, I would encourage you as the husband to pray out loud every time. If your wife is not comfortable praying out loud, give her space and time. As you continue in this approach, you will be modeling for her, and she will likely grow more comfortable in time.

◗ *Focus on the issues of the day.* Voice to the Lord some of the immediate concerns and events facing your lives and family members. What is happening today? Bring before the Lord the concerns of your heart and the issues of life that are at hand.

The timing of God's work in our lives is amazing. On occasion, you go to church, and the message delivered from the Bible is exactly what you need to hear. When that happens, God is speaking to you through the one ministering the Word of God. Similarly, in your prayer journey through God's Word, the Holy Spirit will providentially bring to you and your wife exactly what is relevant for you to pray about. You and your wife will be experiencing God's voice together through His Word—not in a strange mystical experience but in the reality of connecting with one another, with God, and with His Word in prayer.

Here, for example, is how you might use Hebrews 1:1-3 as a Scripture prayer (see Appendix 1 for several other sample Scripture prayers):

HUSBAND: Father, we thank You that in the past You have spoken to us by our fathers through the prophets in portions and in many ways. But Lord, we thank You that we live in the last days, during which You have spoken to us through Your Son, Jesus Christ! We thank You that Jesus has been appointed heir of all things. We thank You that You have created the universe through Jesus.

WIFE: The Son is the radiance of God's glory and the exact representation of His being. We thank You that Jesus sustains all things by His powerful Word. We praise You that Jesus has provided purification for our sins and that He is now seated at the right hand of the Majesty in heaven. And we thank You that Jesus is superior to any and all of the angels and that He has inherited a name that is superior to the name of any angel!

A prayer like this is voiced, not "off the top of your head" but rather from following very words of the Bible.

Important Questions

1. When are my wife and I going to do this?

You need to discover what works for your marriage and family. For some couples, the early morning is good. For others, praying together in the evening or just before bedtime is best. One of you may be a morning person and the other a night person, so you will need to experiment with different options. There are no formulas here. I often tell men, "You just have to figure it out. You solve difficult problems at work. You can solve this challenge at home."

2. How much time should we take?
This prayer time is typically short, recognizing that you face the pressures of a daily schedule. Again, you need to determine what works for you and your wife. On the other hand, there will be times when you and your wife are not in a hurry. As the Holy Spirit leads you, and the discussion flows, you may be shocked at how the time will fly. Right now you might not be able to imagine spending an hour or more in prayer and spiritual discussion with your wife. As you *Just Say the Word* together, a wonderful, extended season of prayer with your wife could be right around the corner!

3. What if we miss?
Oh, to be sure, you will miss. Life can be crazy. In this generation, we are moving faster than mankind has ever moved. We are like Superman: "faster than a speeding bullet." I imagine you would agree that the speed of life is at the core of many problems we face. Certainly, it is very easy for the schedules of life to cause you to miss praying together from time to time. Sometimes you may miss several days for one reason or the other. Any combination of things will come up to block you from getting together with your wife for prayer. This is why you both should commit to being intentional about this. While you don't want to be legalistic, you don't want to give yourselves an easy out, either. Two missed days can too easily become three or four—and a sense of

defeat sets in. But guess what? The approach you are engaging with *Just Say the Word* provides the key solution for that as well.

Missing will not lead you to abdication as in the past. Because you are following the Bible as your guide, you will remember exactly where you left off. All you need to do is return to the place in the Bible where you last prayed together. This benefit has blessed my personal experience over and over again. Every occasion when Vicki and I miss praying together—whether it be for one day or many—we can easily ask, "Where did we leave off?" Other men testify to the same advantage. The Bible keeps you on track!

4. How long should we do this?

How about you match the length of commitment you pledged to one another on your wedding day? *Until death do us part.* You and your wife are one-flesh for all of your lives on this side of eternity. Intentional spiritual intimacy around the living Word of God as husband and wife is an anointed expression of your oneness in God for a lifetime.

Key Points to Remember

1. You initiate!

It is important for you as the husband to take the lead. Do *not* wait for your wife to initiate. *You are the one to initiate.* Practice praying the Word yourself, so you have a level of comfort. Ask God to prepare her, to give you the words, the resolve, and determination, to help you both overcome self-

consciousness. Perhaps you will establish a routine
time that will bring you together. But even with
routine, remember that flexibility is important.
Whatever your approach, as her husband, you must
embrace the responsibility to initiate.

2. Be intentional.
Intentionality is the key. As husband, you are the
guardian of this resolution. Think of it this way:
perhaps more intentionally than ever before,
you are stepping forward to be the priest of your
marriage and family. Sometimes a great thing will
occur by accident. But more often than not, great
things become reality because we pursue them
intentionally. Your spiritual leadership is fueled by
your intentionality. You cannot grow in spiritual
leadership by accident.

3. This is not legalism.
Legalism may be described as seeking the approval
and favor of God through following rules and/or
engaging in a certain set of behaviors. With *Just Say
the Word*, you are not establishing a rule for your
lives but rather a healthy and holy routine for your
marriage. You are entering into the very design
and flow of marriage as the three of you come in
union: you, your wife, and God. You are not handing
down a slavish decree for your marriage. You are
establishing a pattern of connecting with the living
God as husband and wife.

JUST SAY THE WORD — A MOVEMENT

We hear about many different movements in our world. There are movements to influence politicians, movements in the medical community to cure chronic illnesses, movements within the missions community. But what movement could powerfully influence marriages, families, the Church, and our society at a most profound and transformational level? It would be movement of husbands who embrace the courage to make a two-fold resolution before God and their wives:

1. Resolve to step into God's design as the spiritual leader of your marriage and family by initiating one-flesh spiritual intimacy with your wife, demonstrated by praying together on a regular basis.

2. Resolve to use the Bible as the guide and template for the content, topics, and flow for your prayers.

Love Your Wife as Christ Loved the Church

Ephesians 5:25-30 says:

Husbands, love your wives, just as Christ also loved the church and gave Himself up for her; that He might sanctify her, having cleansed her by the washing of water with the Word, that He might present to Himself the church in all her glory, having no spot or wrinkle or any such thing, but that she should be holy and blameless.

So husbands ought also to love their own wives as their own bodies. He who loves his own wife love himself; for no one ever hated his own flesh, but nourishes and cherishes it, just as Christ also does the church; because we are members of His body. (NASB)

Look at the main ideas of what Christ did for His Bride, the Church:

- His Motivation—He loved the church;
- His Sacrifice—He gave himself up for her;
- His Purpose—To sanctify and cleanse her;
- His Method—By the washing of water with the Word;
- His Goal—that He might present her to Himself in all her glory, having no spot or wrinkle or any such thing, that she should be holy and blameless.

The apostle Paul uses Jesus' great love and sacrifice for His Bride, the Church, to illustrate the standard of how we are to love our wives. Wow! Have you ever wondered, "How can I love my wife like that?"

My answer? I suggest that your resolve toward leading her in spiritual intimacy is a perfect expression of such love. How loved and valued your wife will feel as you invest this time with her!

Notice, too, that the Bible says Jesus sanctifies His Bride by the "washing of water with the Word." That is exactly *how* you can love your wife. By praying through the Word of God, you will be "washing her with the water of the Word."

Paul calls us to the same expression and model of love: "So husbands ought to love their wives." The New International Version of this scripture says, "In this same way, husbands ought to love their wives as their own bodies. He who loves his wife loves himself." *In this same way* means that Jesus has given us an amazing example of love for His Bride, but also a model to follow. This is so exciting! By the grace of God, I am asking you to join with me and other men in the marriage prayer journey of *Just Say the Word*—to step toward improved spiritual leadership in your marriage. This model is clearly biblical. I also trust you can see that it is simple and do-able.

Is This the Appointed Time for You?

I believe this is a huge decision. In fact, it is potentially a life-transforming decision. I also believe it is not a decision you make on your own. The resolve is of such magnitude that you cannot embrace it apart from the revelation of God calling you to do it. Remember I talked about Habakkuk

2:3, where the prophet says the "revelation awaits the appointed time"?

Here is my question to you: *Is this the appointed time for you?*

It might all seem reasonable, rational, biblical. But does it *grip you*? Is it compelling? Do you sense the Lord is calling you to answer an alarm that has been ringing in your life, maybe for a long time?

If So, Unload Your Burden!

Scores of Christian men are living with the burden of knowing we are failing in spiritual leadership at home. We work on it from time to time, but it doesn't seem to take hold and last.

You may be doing well at church, on the elder or deacon board, on the church staff, in teaching Sunday school, and in other aspects of Christian life and service. Then, from time to time, you hear a message or sermon that convicts you about your lack of spiritual leadership at home. You are exhorted to be a spiritual leader at home. You might even receive some strategic elbow strikes punched in your ribs during the church service. And you feel guilty! You ride home in silence, the burden increased even more. In our bumping along, we have felt defeated. We have not known what to do. But perhaps now God is giving you a clear revelation.

Gentlemen, there is a simple solution right in front of us. In fact, it is so right in front of us that I am amazed I was personally missing it for so long in my own marriage. The answer is in praying the Word of God together.

The truth is I am feeling much better about this part of my marriage and spiritual leadership. Not only is Vicki experiencing blessing and love in a fresh way, but I too am deeply enjoying what the Lord has done in our marriage and spiritual life together. The fact is, I truly miss it when for some reason we are not able to have our prayer time together. We have been learning wonderful truths from the Bible, seeing God bring life and answers to multiple concerns in our lives, family, and ministry. The fingerprints of God have been evident—and we are praising Him for the transformation.

For Young and Old Husbands

Virtually every time I have shared this story with a friend, it pains me to realize I have lost so much time. If you are a young husband, I beg you as a brother ahead of you in the journey of life: Do not continue along as you are and ultimately find yourself with the pain of having failed your wife and family by lack of leadership in prayer.

Seize the opportunity now! Catch the vision now! Invest in the opportunity to provide a one-flesh spiritual umbrella to cover over your marriage, family, and ministry. Pour God's Word over your family—in its principles, values, and truths. The potential fruitfulness in the lives of your children alone is far, far worth it. And even still, in the complexity of life, if you find yourself with a wayward child someday, as we did, you will know you did all you could to pour the Word of God over his or her soul. And that Word will not return void.

We saw this happen in Christina's life in an amazing way.

If you are an older husband, you may have a string of marital years already under your belt. God's alarm has been ringing in your life, and you have been hitting the snooze button over and over. You have lost so much time, as I had. I want to remind you of a spectacular truth of God's kingdom economy: *God is able to restore the years the locusts have eaten* (Joel 2:25). *God makes all things work together for the good for those who love Him, who have been called according to His purpose* (Romans 8:28, NASB). That includes even our losses, which God can transform to become productive in His Kingdom and in our lives. Join the journey of prayer in your marriage and *Just Say the Word*!

Pray through the Book of Philippians

Appendix 3 (page 79) provides a guide you and your wife can use to pray through the book of Philippians. Perhaps praying through the Bible is a fresh idea for you. If so, this guide will help you learn a pattern for observing Prayer Points from the Bible verses to bring your prayers as husband and wife in alignment with God's Word and will. As you and your wife pray through Philippians, you will likely develop a path that will enable you to pray through other books of the Bible as well.

THE THIEF IS AT HAND!

Why does there appear to be widespread abdication by Christian husbands from praying with their wives? It seems making the time to sit down and pray alone with our wives is just not on our radar. Just what is the deal?

We desire to lead the way spiritually for our families, but the path often eludes us. On top of this, there are a variety of reasons we can cite to explain our shortcomings. Although the answers are as complex and varied as the shades on a full-blown color-wheel, here are a few of the reasons floating around in our heads and hearts.

1. "Spiritual leadership was not modeled for me."

Some of us were not raised in homes where we saw a compelling model of spiritual leadership that we could learn to replicate in our own homes. We have been working with no blueprints.

2. "My wife is more spiritual than I am."

This reason abounds. When push comes to shove, many of us recognize that our wives are walking more diligently and intentionally with the Lord than we are. As a result, we are intimidated to presume we have much to add to what she needs.

While there may be some truth in your assessment, it cannot end there. Think of it this way. You don't need to disciple your wife. But regardless, because of God's design, she does need and desire you to lead her spiritually. That is not a contradiction.

   3. "We have tried in the past, but it was not sustainable."

This again is a complicated issue. What did you try? Were you diligent? What caused you to give up and give in? Some of us have tried a variety of methods and models and devotionals provided in the bookstores and at our churches. But it just did not stick.

   The core difference with the *Just Say the Word* prayer journey is that you will be following the Bible as your template. Over time, you will gain momentum and comfort as the Holy Spirit teaches and encourages you and your wife, especially as you see prayers answered. Following the Word of God as our prayer track is biblical, simple, transferable, and sustainable.

   4. "I know that she knows who I really am!"

Tune into this one! As I have talked with men, this seems to be one of the main reasons for our pervasive failure. Men suffer from condemnation, fear, and shame.

   It goes something like this: "My wife knows me so well! She knows all my failures, sins and shortcomings:

- I yell at the kids
- I got us in debt
- I am struggling at work
- I am fighting with my cousin
- I don't keep the house up properly
- I watch the wrong kind of movies
- I have a loose tongue sometimes . . . or all
  the time.

(And the list can go on and on).

"So if I step close to her spiritually and emotionally, it is just too revealing, too shameful. It might even be hypocritical! It is too risky! That close to the light will bring too much exposure!"

Imagine I just yelled at the kids and sent them all to bed, then I am supposed to turn to my wife and say, "OK, honey, let's open the Bible to Proverbs and pray together!" Yeah, right!

So basically we "blow the whistle" and disqualify ourselves. Off to the penalty box we go. The problem is some of us never come out, because we are convinced "I am not good enough to pray with my wife."

My brother, none of us is perfect. But consider this: the answers, motivations, and healing we need can flow from the Word of God as we pray through the truths and principles of Scripture. The most powerful relational union that God intends on earth is husband and wife. There is no other relationship captured in such intimate and personal terms as "one flesh." When we intentionally invite the living God to reside at the center of our marriage, we have access to His life in a unique way. If we step back from the power resident in such a union of prayer, we are losing access to the most powerful resource we have as married men. On the other hand, stepping into this union more intentionally and regularly will open the anointing of God in ways we could not have imagined.

Newsflash #1:
You Are Right—You Are Not "Good Enough"!

And you will *never* be good enough on your own merit. Can you imagine waiting till you finally decide, "OK, I am now 'good enough' to pray with my wife"? How long will that take?

Approaching God is not about our self-righteousness qualifying us. God knows all and sees all. Isaiah 64:6 says, "All of us have become like one who is unclean, and all our righteous acts are like filthy rags; we all shrivel up like a leaf, and like the wind our sins sweep us away." And in the New Testament the Apostle Paul reminds us, "There is no one righteous, not even one" (Romans 3:10).

But God, in His grace, has the solution for our sin crisis. He provided a substitute to take our death penalty: His one and only Son, the Lord Jesus Christ. Isaiah 53:6 declares, "We all, like sheep, have gone astray, each of us has turned to his own way; and the Lord has laid on him the iniquity of us all."

Thank God for allowing us the *Great Exchange*: "God made Him who had no sin to be sin for us, so that in Him we might become the righteousness of God" (2 Corinthians 5:21). This is the heart of the Gospel of Jesus Christ. God laid upon His Son our sin debt and gave us in exchange His righteousness.

It is only the righteousness of Jesus Christ that qualifies us for eternal salvation. In the same way, our qualification to come before God in prayer is not because of who we are but because of who we are *in His Son Jesus Christ*. Please remember to tell yourself: You are not disqualified from praying with your wife. Unworthy? Yes! Disqualified? No! (And remember: No matter how highly you regard your wife, her own righteousness doesn't make her "good enough" either!)

Newsflash #2:
The Thief Comes Only to Steal, Kill, and Destroy.

John 10:10 proclaims, "The thief comes only to steal and kill and destroy; I have come that they may have life, and have it to the full."

Jesus refers to the devil as a thief. He is a murderous, destructive *thief*. His schemes are always designed to take away what is best from us and our families. That is his only agenda.

When the enemy can convince you that you are disqualified from praying with your wife, he tricks you into stepping away from the one of most powerful resources you have in your life: one-flesh spiritual intimacy. With this subtle scheme he "steals, kills and destroys" vast fruitfulness from your life and family.

But the devil is disarmed when we fight with the Word of God. This is the same strategy Jesus used against Satan during His temptations in the wilderness.

Imagine this vivid scene. If you knew a literal thief was coming to your home to ravage your wife, harm your children, and steal your things, you would rise to the occasion to resist him with all your power. Well, gentlemen, *the thief is at hand!*

Most often the thief does not come crashing in loudly and forcefully. More commonly he works slowly, robbing God of His glory and taking joy from your marriage and family.

Protect Your Family with Prayer

Do not listen to the accuser. Do not allow the enemy to shame you into opting out of the most powerful resource in your life and marriage. Determine to step up to your role as spiritual leader in your marriage and family. By praying the Bible with your wife, you will be equipped to fight the good fight as never before. The heart of a husband and father innately beats with a commitment to provide for and protect his wife and children.

This is the core of the *Just Say the Word* challenge. In our generation, marriage and family are under severe pressure. It is a war for the souls of our children! Life for them is not as it was when you and I grew up. The thief wants especially to target children, teens, and young adults. As fathers, you and I have the responsibility to not only protect them as best we can physically but spiritually as well. Can you think of a better way to cover your family spiritually than to pray over them a consistent diet of God's living Word?

Stand Up and Step Forward

Don't wait till you feel you have arrived at some place of worthiness before you stand up and step forward into your design for spiritual leadership. The growing answers and resources for your life and family are found in the journey. We frequently would prefer that God show up *first*. Then we can move forward with confidence. But the Kingdom of God normally works in paradox—in the opposite way to natural thinking. In His Kingdom, God prefers us to trust Him and press forward by faith, and *then* He shows up.

DISTURBING RESPONSES

"Suppose your wife were sitting here right now. If we told her you have made a decision to step into this commitment to meet together with her on a reasonably regular basis—to read some of the Bible and pray together, using the Bible text as a guide to pray over your family and some immediate needs—*what would she say*?"

I've asked that question many times, and I've heard a couple of revealing responses.

She would say, "I've heard this before!" (Imagine her saying this with a furrowed brow.)

Here is another one: "I'm not sure my wife even wants to pray with me."

What do these responses say to you?

I have challenged my friends who are facing such situations with this thought:

You really need to press in. Ask God to help you. You need to win your wife all over again in this area of spiritual and emotional life together. Sounds like you have failed her, as I was failing my wife. Determine not to fail her again. Position your resolve *before God*, not just before your wife. If she has a cool response to

your new commitment, receive that as
a clear signal you must press in all the
more to the prayer journey and *Just Say
the Word.*

A More Difficult Marriage

Perhaps this whole discussion is painful to you
because your marriage is in a difficult place. Maybe
your wife will not agree to pray through the Bible
with you. If that's the case, then I call you to "press
into the Lord" even more firmly. You can personally
follow this approach on your own. In fact, there
is nothing better you can do in the midst of such
challenges than to pray the Word of God for your
wife, for your family, and for yourself!

Because of who you are in her life, as her
husband, you have the opportunity to pray more
effectively for her than anyone else. You might have a
hard time believing that, but it is true.

One friend said that some issues made it
uncomfortable for his wife to pray out loud with him.
However, she would allow him to pray with her. So
he did just that. In short order he testified, "Praying
for my wife has changed me!"

"A Revolution in Our Marriage"

One man in a tough situation has come
back to me and exclaimed:

Sam, this has been a revolution in our marriage! I have tried to initiate some spiritual things before with my wife—read a booklet together, a prayer devotional, or a marriage book with questions to be answered—but really it has never worked. So we have not been doing anything together. But now reading together and praying through the Bible is comfortable. This works! I tried other things in the past, but they just did not work for us. Praying the Bible does.

This friend told me so many good things over a lunch that I was scribbling notes on a napkin, but I couldn't keep up. He was going on and on about what this new journey of prayer has done for his marriage. He has finally answered the alarm!

JOURNEYING TOGETHER

A friend emailed, "I know, for me, if I hear a challenge like this, and I say to myself, 'I'm in,' it may or may not last. However, if I tell someone else 'I'm in,' then I will have a brother that I will also be accountable to." He is right on the mark!

A critical part of *Just Say the Word* is going on this journey together with other men who share the same resolve. Of course, you will primarily be accountable to God and to your wife. Obviously, she will know if you follow through or not. But you do not want her to be in the position of holding your feet to the fire. You really need other men who are also committed to the journey to help hold you accountable.

Journeying together with a friend or a group of men is a huge asset for your resolve. I have no idea how you came across this book. Perhaps the friend who recommended it would be a partner to share the journey with you. But please do not embark on this path alone. You need other married men to co-own the resolve.

I do not advocate an overbearing system of checking up on one another, however. Such efforts only produce a legalistic and rote following, and it fails the very spirit of *Just Say the Word*. You don't need another thing to check off your to-do list, just so you can say, "I did it."

What each of us needs is a band of "mighty men" who seek to be powerful in the economy of God's Kingdom. We need a friend, or several friends, who can help us through the realities of life, who will pray for us as we pray for them. Hebrews 10:24-25 comes to mind:

> And let us consider how we may spur one another on toward love and good deeds. Let us not give up meeting together, as some are in the habit of doing, but let encourage one another— and all the more as you see the Day approaching.

Not long ago, I shared the *Just Say the Word* challenge with a gathering of men on a Saturday morning at a local church. Nearing the conclusion, I asked the men to simply put their name, email address, and wife's name on a notecard if they felt led to step toward the marriage prayer journey. Suddenly, almost pre-emptively, a man stood up and walked forward to personally hand me his notecard. He then turned to his Christian brothers and said, "Men, I needed to hear this challenge! I also know I need to be held accountable. So I am going to write my name on the whiteboard, and if you want to be held accountable as well, you too come write your name." From that moment, during our closing prayer, and continuing afterwards, man after man, made his way forward to pen his name publicly! It was a brave gesture by that first man. But he "got it," and he stepped forward to call for commitment. He knew the only way he would find success was if he could journey together, not only with his wife, but also with a band of likeminded brothers.

It is not good to go alone. Over and over, the Bible shows God sending men forward, not only with His presence, but side-by-side with other men. Each of our lives represents a door, which can swing open to influence others. Who can you influence to press into more intentional and regular spiritual leadership in his marriage? Can you think of the name of another husband whom you believe needs to hear this challenge? Can you think of 3 to 5 other husbands? How about 10 others? These potentially are the men with whom you can journey so as to encourage one another.

Church—a House of Prayer

Think about your local church family. Can you imagine the impact in the marriages, families, and ministries of your local church, if the *Just Say the Word* prayer journey were to be in the DNA of each Christian husband?

Jesus talked about the gathering of His people into the temple designed to be a "house of prayer." He is not talking about a program of prayer. He is talking about the nature, character, and spirit of His people as they assemble. I believe this very dynamic is within the reach of our churches today. But it cannot start at the church. It needs to start in our homes!

The only way for this movement to reach its fullness in our homes is for Christian husbands and fathers to seize the opportunity to offer God's Word prayerfully over their marriages and families. Perhaps you can begin a movement to influence the

Christian husbands in your church. We will never have a house of prayer at the corporate church level until we have "houses of prayer" in our homes. Houses of prayer scattered become a House of Prayer gathered.

You can share this challenge with other men in your sphere of influence at church or work. How about at your men's group? Sunday school class? Discipleship group? The Lord can use you to call other men to join you on this journey. I believe with all my heart that the scope of fruitfulness and transformation that you can effect is likely beyond what you could ask or imagine.

Treasure and Pearls

The kingdom of heaven is like treasure hidden in a field. When a man found it, he hid it again, and then in his joy went and sold all he had and bought that field. Again, the kingdom of heaven is like a merchant looking for fine pearls. When he found one of great value, he went away and sold everything he had and bought it. (Matthew 13:44-46)

These two parables by Jesus are among His shortest, but they are packed with meaning. Even though they seem very similar, there are some key differences between them. The first man is an ordinary field worker, going about his daily work. He is not searching or seeking for anything special. He has no sense of expectancy. He is simply going about the routine of life. Then suddenly he makes the amazing and completely unexpected discovery of a treasure.

The merchant, on the other hand, is quite different. He is a businessman on a daily and diligent search for precious pearls. He arises every morning thinking about pearls. Perhaps he even dreams of pearls at night. He believes with all his heart there are pearls "out there" to be acquired, and he is diligently searching for them. On this fateful day, he finally discovers the pearl of a lifetime.

To summarize these stories, here are a few observations:

- Each man made a discovery.
- Each quickly assessed the value of what he found.
- Each man clearly made a decision to acquire his discovery.
- Each man took sacrificial action to become the owner of his find.

In these parables, Jesus shows us that whether or not we are intentionally seeking His treasure, God is a Revealer, and in His timing, He is capable of revealing the "treasure and pearls" of His Kingdom.

When God convicted me through the heartfelt challenge from my wife, I soon discovered that He was actually showing me a kingdom treasure. To tell you the truth, I was not really looking for it. I was like the ordinary field worker.

How would you characterize yourself? Are you the field worker or the merchant? Are you plodding along faithfully in your routine? Or are you on a search mission? Think through where you are, and ask yourself the following questions:

- Do you recognize the *Just Say the Word* marriage prayer journey as a discovery from God? Is this a revelation at the appointed time for you as a treasure or a pearl?
- Do you see tremendous potential and value for your life, marriage, and family?
- Are you willing to make a decision to step toward owning this treasure/pearl?
- And most importantly, are you willing take the personal, sacrificial actions needed to obtain them?

Discovery. Value. Decision. Sacrifice.

Your first step forward can be the hardest. And I can promise you that the first step will not be your last step. The steps are a call to the journey of a lifetime of spiritual leadership in your marriage and home.

Acquiring great value is worth great sacrifice. The value is in the possibilities, opportunities, and fruitfulness, which can exceed all we could ask for or imagine.

Yet sacrificial action does not happen accidentally. It can *only* be intentional. In each parable, the man "went and sold all he had." What sacrifices do you need to make to lay down your life for your wife, as Christ did for His Bride, the Church?

The ultimate example is Jesus Christ. Jesus *discovered a mission* in the eternal will of God the Father. He recognized the *great value* in reconciling our souls to God and the entire creation which groans under the curse of sin. Jesus *embraced a decision* as He prayed, "Not my will, but Thy will be done." And He took *sacrificial action* as He offered Himself as the eternal sacrifice for our sins on the cross.

Filled with Hope

The beauty and power of this model is that I have seen it give hope to many men. They say to me, "You know, I believe I can do this!" And they're right. This is a way to stay on track by following the Bible in your prayers with your wife.

I wish there was a way to sit with each of you personally to talk through this challenge. Since that is impossible, I pray God will energize this form of communicating with you. I pray you will answer God's alarm. Quit hitting the snooze button. Get out of bed, put your feet on the floor, and start walking by the grace of God!

I am asking you to *Just Say the Word* and start the prayer journey with your wife immediately. Send your name, email address, and your wife's name to me at contact@justsaytheword.net. Vicki and I will pray for you and your wife. Also, from time to time I send out a brief message to this band of brothers/husbands as a reminder of the challenge, with ideas, exhortations, and testimonies of encouragement.

> *You can do this! And I am sure God will go with you.*

Now to Him who is able to do immeasurably more than all we ask or imagine, according to His power that is at work within us, to Him be glory in the church and in Christ Jesus throughout all generation, for ever and ever! Amen! (Ephesians 3:20-21)

SAMPLE SCRIPTURE PRAYERS

Guiding Thoughts

Turn in your Bible and follow along as we pray these passages. Of course, there are many versions of the Bible, but that does not matter. For the passages in this appendix, I use the *New International Version*.

Scripture praying simply allows the Bible to show you what to pray. There are many times when Vicki and I follow the exact text of the verses, but we are not reading them, we are *praying* them.

There really is no wrong way to do this. The more you do it, the more comfortable you will become.

Several Suggestions

In Scripture praying, you can mark up your Bible, or you may want to have a pen and pad of paper nearby to jot notes. I've listed below how you might want to proceed.

> **Read** the whole passage you desire to pray through. Don't take too many verses at a time. Take turns reading the Bible, or approach it in whatever way is more workable for your marriage.

▶ **Think** about the verses for a few minutes. This is the time during which the Holy Spirit will show you and your wife the main ideas, words, topics, and concepts in this passage.

▶ **Share briefly** with one another what you observe and/or what you sense you are hearing from the Holy Spirit. I prefer to allow my wife to share first. And remember, this is not a teaching and Bible study time. It's a prayer time!

▶ **What key words or ideas** jump out at you? Mark them in your Bible or jot them down on a piece of paper. Look for things to pray for yourselves and your children. Tune in to things to thank God for, or for things that would lead you to worship and praise Him.

▶ **Pray to the Lord** as you follow the flow of the verses. Mention to the Lord key words, ideas, phrases, topics, and content straight from the Bible. You and your wife can take turns praying. Just be sure to proceed in whatever way is most comfortable for your marriage. As you move along the prayer journey, you will both find increasing comfort and confidence in your communication with one another and with the Lord.

Example from the Epistles, following the text of Colossians 1:9-14

HUSBAND: Father in heaven, we thank You today for Your Word. We thank You that we can use Your Word not only as Scripture to read and study, but as a living guide to help understand You and Your Kingdom. We are blessed that we have Your Word as a guide we can follow for our prayers.

Many times we feel like we don't even know what to pray. Many times we wander or get lost in our prayers. But following Your Word can help my wife and me to know exactly how to pray Your will and truths. We ask You, Father, for me and my wife and our children, that You would fill us with the knowledge of Your will through all spiritual wisdom and understanding. We pray that we would be able to live lives worthy of the Lord and pleasing in every way.

WIFE: Lord, help us to bear fruit in every good work that You have set before us. Help us grow in our knowledge of Who you are. Strengthen us with all Your power according to Your glorious might. Lord, help us to have great endurance and patience. Fill us in such a way that we will joyfully give thanks to You.

We are reminded today from Your Word that You have qualified us to share in the inheritance of the saints in the kingdom of light. We thank You for the truth that we have been rescued from the dominion of darkness and brought into the kingdom of the Son whom You love, in whom we have redemption and forgiveness of our sins. Amen.

Example from the Gospels, following the story of the paralyzed man lowered through the roof to Jesus in Mark 2:1-12

HUSBAND: Father in heaven, we thank You for the life of the Lord Jesus Christ! We thank You that You sent Him from heaven to do many wonderful miracles, and that these great miracles are the evidence that everything He said is true.

We thank You for the miracle in this wonderful story in the Gospel of Mark. This story tells us the power of Jesus Christ was so evident that people were clamoring to come to Him for healing and for help. Thank You for the great faith of these four men who were willing to step outside their comfort zones and embrace the spirit of endurance and faith, to dig a hole through the roof, and lower their friend before the Lord Jesus.

WIFE: Lord, this paralyzed man could not help himself. We don't know if he was a friend or a relative of these other four men. But we see that these men cared for him, and they all believed something very good about Jesus Christ. They believed that if they could carry their friend to Jesus, something good would happen. Lord, verse five says that when Jesus "saw their faith," He said, "My son, your sins are forgiven." Help us to have that kind of faith.

Lord, we know Jesus is looking for faith. We know You want us and our children to be strong in faith. Lord, we pray today that when Jesus looks upon our lives He will see our faith. We pray that You will strengthen our faith today. May our faith be of the same quality as these men who carried their paralyzed friend to Jesus. We are reminded in this passage that Jesus has the authority on earth to forgive sins. And not only the sins of the world, but our sins as individuals! We praise You for this great reality, the forgiveness of sins. That is what this story is really all about. Not only about healing the paralyzed man, but Jesus' authority to do something we cannot see with our eyes: to forgive this man's sins.

HUSBAND: Lord, remind us today that we are like the paralyzed man. Apart from You, we cannot walk at all. We thank You that we have received by faith the forgiveness of our sins from the Lord Jesus Christ. We thank God for this great gift! We pray that the knowledge and certainty of this special and eternal gift will strengthen our faith. Help us to be on watch for "paralyzed people" around us, people who cannot walk in some aspect of their lives. Help us to know how we can help carry them to Jesus. Amen.

Example from the Psalms following the text of Psalm 23:1-3

The Psalms fall in the poetry section of the Bible. They were ancient songs and are now wonderful guides for our prayers because they touch on such a wide range of emotions and issues of life.

HUSBAND: Heavenly Father, we thank You today that we can take confidence in this great truth from Your Word that the Lord is my Shepherd. Of course, it is true that the Lord is the Shepherd of all His sheep. But today we rejoice that You are our

Shepherd.

We thank You that, because You are God, we are not lost in the large flock, but You know and care for us as individuals, as a married couple, and as a family. We are reminded today of all the wonderful things a shepherd provides for his sheep. He guides them. He leads them to pasture. He leads them to water. He keeps them from enemies, and he cares for them in every way. Because the Lord is our Shepherd, we are reminded today that we shall not be in want. The Shepherd knows our needs, and in this we can take a rest.

WIFE: We thank You that the Shepherd leads us to lie down in green pastures, that He leads us beside quiet waters. Father, in the place of green pastures and quiet waters, our souls can be restored. Lord, sometimes our souls go through many struggles and much turmoil. We are, in fact, experiencing unrest in our minds and our emotions today because of the troubles and pressures we face. So we ask you today, good Shepherd, to take us to the green, quiet place for restoration.

Thank You for guiding us in the paths of righteousness for Your Name's sake. We are reminded that You want us to walk in the path of righteousness. And this righteousness is not only for our good and joy, but it is for the sake of Your Name!

HUSBAND: Fill our lives to be a testimony of Your righteousness. On our own and in our own resources, we are insufficient to be a proper witness for You. Lord, I ask You as the good Shepherd to fill us in such a way that Your righteousness will be evident. Fill us up so we will continue to take rest and be nurtured in the green pastures and to drink beside the quiet waters. We are blessed to be reminded today, that You, Lord, are our Shepherd! Amen.

Example from the Proverbs

HUSBAND: Heavenly Father, we thank You so much for the gift of the children You have given to us. We count it a privilege and responsibility to come before Your throne of grace on their behalf. We know the wisdom and the truths in the book of Proverbs represent wonderful guidance on how we, as parents, can pray over our children and for their futures. We pray for our children, that they would not forget the teachings we have given them, but that they would keep them bound up in their hearts. We ask that these teachings would prolong their lives for many years and bring them prosperity according to your will.

WIFE: Lord, we pray that love and faithfulness will never leave their lives. We pray love and faithfulness will be bound around their necks and written as a tablet upon their hearts. We pray to You, God, that our children would win Your favor and a good name with both God and man. Lord, we pray that our children would trust in You with all their hearts and that they would not lean on their own understanding. We pray that in all their ways they will acknowledge You and You will therefore make their paths straight.

We are reminded in these proverbs that You desire that our hearts and all of our ways belong to

You. Anything less than 100 percent commitment to You does not make sense because You are God!

HUSBAND: Help our children not to give in to the deception of becoming wise in their own eyes. Rather, we ask that they would fear the Lord first in their lives! We also ask that they would have the wisdom and perspective to shun evil. We pray, God, that the truth of Your Word would be bound up in their hearts and that Your truth would bring health to their bodies and nourishment to their bones. We pray that they would learn to honor the Lord with the first fruits of their wealth and that their barns would be filled to overflowing because of Your gracious provision. Amen.

JUST SAY THE WORD
TESTIMONIES

Here are some testimonies from men who have decided to *Just Say the Word*. They are journeying together to embrace intentional spiritual intimacy with their wives, particularly by praying through the Bible together.

Thanks for stepping out on this, Sam. It is much needed in my marriage as I suspect those of other men I know. My wife and I started regular prayer together over a year ago, and it is a life changer. It certainly helps take marriage to the next level. We have floundered a bit in finding something to center our time around, and your suggestion of praying the Bible seems spot on. Today will be our first, and I have a good feeling about it going well. I intend to take this to the men of our church in the next 2 months. I want some time under my belt so I can personally recommend the process (using the Bible as a couples' prayer tool) with credibility. Will let you know how it goes.

Thanks again for pressing ahead and sharing.

We started this morning!

My couples community group met last night and I felt led by the SPIRIT to share your challenge with the 4 men in our group. They were grateful for the challenge and openly confessed their lack of spiritual leadership in their relationships with their wives. I've asked them to pray about taking the "challenge" and let me know if they're willing to be held accountable to the commitment. Based on their reactions and response, I'm sure we will soon have 4 more men more intentionally seeking to be one with their wives in giving their marriages to GOD.

Thanks again for your transparency and leadership and may GOD continue to bless you and guide you.

Sam - Thanks so much for sharing this with us this morning. This has been an area of struggle for me for many years. Knowing that other leaders struggle in the area is huge for me. Needless to say, I want to join The Prayer Journey.

My wife and I started praying together last Friday night and have done it each night since. We are starting with the book of James. Wonderful experience so far. We are also using the time to pray for our son. I had been hitting the "snooze button" over the past few months regarding praying for our young son. I think in part because I couldn't get my arms around all that there was to pray about. I was having trouble figuring out a place to start. I now believe that praying the Bible was the perfect way to start. Using the first chapter of James as our guide, my wife and I have prayed about some pretty deep stuff for our son over the past few nights.

Thanks for taking time out to come over and share what God's laid on your heart. Joy and I are going *to give praying through Scripture a shot as a way to keep our time together fresh. I really appreciate the <u>profound simplicity</u> of the approach and look forward to giving it a go!*

We're off and running! We've started in James and are taking it a couple verses at a time. Like you said, nothing fancy. Just using the passage as a template for the prayer. I'll let you know how it's going once we've been at it for a while.

My wife and I have been praying nearly every day (about 13 days since you and I met) through Nehemiah. I've actually been amazed at listening to how and what she prays about. Her perspective is different but very complementary, and she's told me how much she enjoys these prayer times. I'm still amazed that we haven't been doing this sooner.

Shared with my wife yesterday my commitment, and she was overjoyed. She is currently going through a course right now with her Bible study group that is teaching to read, ponder, and pray through Scripture, so it is very timely. She and I have committed to pray for the next day about what book we should start with and begin tomorrow morning. Thank you for your obedience in this calling to share this with other men. I am looking forward to keeping you posted on our progress.

For me, it has now been four days of praying with my wife. It is something that I have to be very intentional about. Monday was very "stiff." Tuesday,

*it was very convicting for me. I had to apologize
about some things. Each day it has been more
comfortable. I'll pray for you and ask that you pray
for me as we walk through this challenge together for
our marriage sake. For God's Glory and for HIS Fame.*

*Thank you, Sam, for sharing your heart with
the Marriage Prayer Testimony. Hearing of your
experience really pierced my heart, and I knew that
before I went to bed last night that I had to share your
story with my wife. You see, I too had to confess my
failure as the Spiritual Leader of our home. We had
a wonderful time talking through the issues, and we
are now committed more than ever to pray on a daily
basis. I also want you to know that I come in contact
with many married men at my church, and I plan on
sharing your testimony with as many as I possibly can.
I will keep you updated on my progress.*

*Started last week. 4 out of 7! Feel free to check in
with me from time to time : -)*

*We have been praying nightly consistently – been
through Philippians, Colossians and now in Ephesians 6.*

PRAYING THROUGH PHILIPPIANS

The purpose of *Just Say the Word* is to present a model of prayer that enables husbands and wives to pray together more consistently and effectively. Because the Bible is the living and active word of God, praying through scripture becomes a practical way to draw God's Word into your life, marriage, and family. The plan in this appendix will help you and your wife pray through the book of Philippians.

Here's the pattern you'll follow:
- Read each selection of verses.
- Meditate on what you have read, listening for the Holy Spirit to speak to your hearts.
- Each of you shares your observations. Remember, this is not a time for Bible teaching; it is a time of prayer.
- Allow the Bible to reveal what to pray for your individual lives, marriage, children, church, ministry, and career. Also pray for other people as God leads you, weaving in the Prayer Points that may apply. The Prayer Points are simply suggestions from the passage to help guide your prayers.

PHILIPPIANS PRAYER GUIDE

Read Philippians 1:1-6

Prayer Points:

Jesus Christ is Lord! We are servants and saints in Christ Jesus. Grace and peace comes from God our Father. Express thankfulness for your spouse, children, and others who come to mind. We praise God for the blessing of being partakers and partners in the Gospel. Thank God today for the person who shared the Gospel with you. We are confident of God's work in our lives from the first day until now—and until the day of Christ Jesus!

Read Philippians 1:7-11

Prayer Points:

We are called to defend and confirm the Gospel. Many Christians suffer for the Gospel in chains of oppression and persecution. Pray for their strength and resolve. Pray for Christ's affection to become real in your own hearts. Pray for your love to abound and to align with the truth and to have depth of insight. God helps us to discern what is best so that we might be pure, blameless, and filled with the fruit of righteousness to the glory and praise of God.

Read Philippians 1:12-14

Prayer Points:
Pray for the advance of the Gospel in our generation. Who can you influence for the Gospel among your family, friends, neighbors, co-workers, etc.? Call out the names of three of these people, and pray that the Lord will prepare their hearts for the message of Christ. Ask God to fill you both with boldness, that you may become more intentional in sharing the Gospel through your spheres of influence. Pray for confidence to speak courageously and fearlessly! And pray for those who are persecuted and even chained for the Gospel today.

Read Philippians 1:15-18

Prayer Points:
We must guard against envy and rivalry in our hearts. Even when there are disagreements among God's children, the important thing is that Christ is preached. The Lord God knows the motives of our hearts—some are false but others are true. Pray that God gives you the resolve to defend the Gospel at every opportunity. Has trouble been stirred up for you because of the Gospel? Pray that the Lord will help you to stand firm together—and continue to rejoice!

Read Philippians 1:19-21

Prayer Points:

Our prayers matter. They influence people's lives—especially our own children! God has given us a beautiful provision in the Holy Spirit. He is at work in our lives and in those we pray for. Lift up the names of your children and other family who are on your heart today. Pray that Christ will be exalted in your body, whether by life or by death, that He give you courage, and that you not be ashamed of your faith. "For me to live is Christ, and to die is gain!"

Read Philippians 1:22-26

Prayer Points:

Pray for fruitful labor for Jesus Christ to be manifest in your lives, marriage, children, and church. Praise God for the confidence He gives concerning your eternal future with Christ. Ultimately, to be with Christ is the destiny of every Christian, which Paul reminds us will be far better than this world. Pray for progress and joy in your personal faith and the faith of those you love. Our lives can cause others to have joy and to boast in Jesus Christ!

Read Philippians 1:27-30

Prayer Points:
Pray to make intentional choices to conduct your life and marriage worthy of the Gospel of Christ. Ask the Lord to enable you to stand firm in one spirit in your marriage, working together for the faith of the Gospel. Pray that you can stand without being frightened by those who oppose the Gospel. The Word says those who oppose the Gospel will be destroyed, but God will save believers. Even though we believe in Jesus and our salvation is sure, we may yet be called to suffer and struggle for Christ and His Gospel. How might you be suffering for Jesus Christ? What struggles do you face right now because of your commitment to Jesus Christ and His kingdom?

Read Philippians 2:1-5

Prayer Points:
May your marriage draw encouragement from being united with Christ, comforted by His love and in fellowship with His Spirit. Pray for tenderness and compassion, joy, like-mindedness, the same love, and to be one in spirit and purpose. Do nothing out of selfish ambition or vain conceit. Pray for humility that will enable you to consider others better than yourselves—in your marriage, among your children, within the members of your extended family and church family. Pray that you will look not just to your own interests but to the interests of others. What are some "interests of others" that you can pray about

and act upon? Ask God for the mindset of Christ Jesus.

Read Philippians 2:6-11

Prayer Points:

Glorify the name and person of Jesus Christ! Jesus in His very nature is God. We confess what the Bible says: Jesus did not consider equality with God something to be grasped. He made Himself nothing and took the very nature of a servant, made in human likeness. Praise God for sending His Son! Jesus humbled Himself and became obedient to death on the cross, and God exalted Jesus to the highest place. Jesus' name is above every name. Confess that every knee will bow in heaven and on earth. Today, let your tongues confess that Jesus is Lord, to the glory of God the Father!

Read Philippians 2:12-16

Prayer Points:

We are called to live in obedience as children and servants of God. The reality of salvation should be evident in our lives. God is working in us to will and to act according to His good purpose. Do everything without complaining or arguing.

Pray that in your marriage you will be blameless, that you will be pure children of God, without fault in a crooked and depraved generation. May you shine as stars in the universe, holding firmly to the

Word of life, and may you be able to boast on the day of Christ that you did not run or labor in vain.

Read Philippians 2:17-21

Prayer Points:

Our lives are to be poured out like a drink offering, a sacrifice and service to the Lord with rejoicing and gladness. Timothy was a great example of selfless service. About whom can you say: "I have no one else like him"? Lift up the names of these dear friends to the Lord. May you take genuine interest in other people and their families. While it is natural to prioritize and focus on your own interests, pray for something new and fresh to take hold in your hearts. Pray that the things that interest Jesus Christ will be the priority interests in your marriage and family.

Read Philippians 2:22-24

Prayer Points:

Paul was blessed as Timothy proved himself in the faith and service of Christ. They served together as a spiritual son and father. In our generation, the work of the Gospel is crucial and deserves our attention and participation. Yet the work of the kingdom is not something we do on our own, but together with others. With whom do you serve in your church and/or community? Call out the names of these people in your prayers today. Pray for your pastor and his family.

Read Philippians 2:25-30

Prayer Points:
Epaphroditus was a brother, fellow worker, fellow soldier, and messenger. God has placed us in those same roles. Epaphroditus was an amazing example by his personal sacrifices for God's people and work in the kingdom. When you think of sacrificial service, who comes to your minds today? These verses recall to us that even faithful workers for God struggle and suffer, so remember God always has a bigger picture in mind than what we see from our earthly perspective.

Read Philippians 3:1-6

Prayer Points:
Self-righteousness and religion can cause anyone to stumble spiritually. Paul was a high-level Jewish leader and teacher who performed all the proper religious duties and more. He placed his trust in his own good works and in his religious position. Yet Paul had an awakening. May you, too, remember that we serve God by His Spirit. We boast only in Christ Jesus and must not put one ounce of confidence in our flesh and good works. No one can earn favor with God by religious activities and legalism. Obedience to Jesus Christ is not for our glory but for His alone!

Read Philippians 3:7-11

Prayer Points:
Whatever we may regard as personal gain for ourselves, we are to consider it garbage for the sake of Jesus Christ. Surpassing worth lies in knowing Christ Jesus as our Lord! Seek to gain Christ in your marriage and to be found in Him together. Righteousness does not come from following the law. True righteousness comes only from God on the basis of faith in Jesus Christ. May you grow in your knowledge of Christ and the power of Jesus who is living His resurrected life in each of your lives. As Jesus was raised from the dead, you will be raised to eternal life!

Read Philippians 3:12-14

Prayer Points:
Paul's testimony inspires us to grow spiritually and seek to fulfill God's will. Believe God has a secure hold on your marriage and family, and ask God to enable you to fulfill His purposes for your lives together. Pray the same truth over the lives of your children. May you learn to move beyond the past and strain toward what is ahead. Press toward the goal, to win the prize for which God has called you heavenward!

Read Philippians 3:15-16

Prayer Points:
Spiritual maturity knows that God's righteousness comes from faith in Jesus Christ, not from religious works and obeying the law. Maturity is further evident when we seek to fulfill the purposes God has designed for our lives and marriage. Pray for increasing spiritual clarity to understand how God is working in your lives, marriage, and children. Pray that you will live up to what you already know of God's Word, will, and purposes.

Read Philippians 3:17-21

Prayer Points:
People can serve as godly examples for one another. Pray to model Christ for each other in your marriage and also in the eyes of your children. Truly there are enemies of the cross of Christ destined for destruction. Their minds are set on earthly things. Praise God for the reality that your citizenship is in heaven, and praise the Lord Jesus Christ who has the power to bring everything under His control. With this same power, Jesus will transform our bodies to become like His glorious body!

Read Philippians 4:1-3

Prayer Points:

We are reminded again in Philippians that it is important and possible to stand firm in the Lord. What does standing firm mean for your lives and marriage at this time? In what relationships do you need God's grace to help stand? Euodia and Syntyche disagreed over some issues that resulted in tension. Yet even those whose names are written in heaven and who work for the Gospel can be in disagreement with one another. Communication is vital if unity is to be gained. May the Lord equip you to manage differences with love and wisdom.

Read Philippians 4:4-6

Prayer Points:

Rejoice in the Lord . . . always! May gentleness take hold and become evident in your marriage. Praise the Lord for the truth of His nearness to your lives and to your children. Worry and anxiety are regular struggles for our souls, but the Bible exhorts us not to be anxious about anything. Turn over your struggles to the Lord. In everything, by your prayers and petitions, with thanksgiving, present your requests to God. Thank Him for the momentum and fruit of praying together more intentionally and more regularly using the Bible as your guide.

Read Philippians 4:7-9

Prayer Points:

The peace of God is a wonderful reality that transcends all understanding. Pray the peace of God will guard your hearts and minds as never before. May your minds be occupied by whatever is true, noble, right, pure, lovely, admirable, excellent, and praiseworthy. May you see what God sees. Pray over the minds of your family members to be captured by thinking on such things, and the God of peace will be with you.

Read Philippians 4:10-13

Prayer Points:

Contentment is often elusive in our culture and generation. Greed and jealousy reign. Pray to guard your hearts from these insidious sins and to learn contentment in whatever your circumstances—whether in plenty or in need. The secret of contentment is to know that you can do all things through Christ who gives you strength. May the Lord strengthen your marriage and children regardless of circumstances to give you supernatural contentment and peace.

Read Philippians 4:14-17

Prayer Points:

It is good to pay attention to the troubles of others. Earlier in Philippians, we were challenged to look not only to our own interests but also to the interests of others. The Philippians looked out for the concerns and needs of Paul and his ministry. How can you serve someone who is in need—particularly those who are ministering for the Gospel? Not only are the recipients blessed by your attention and generosity, but also your gifts of love are credited by God to your account for reward and blessing—both in this life and in eternity.

Read Philippians 4:18-23

Prayer Points:

Gifts of love which help meet others' needs are fragrant offerings and acceptable sacrifices that please God. Pray for balance in your hearts about focusing on your needs and the needs of others. Whom do you know that has a need right now? As you are concerned with the needs of others, the Lord God will supply all your needs according to His glorious riches in Christ Jesus. Glory to God the Father forever and ever!

Keep Going

Congratulations! You and your wife have perhaps for the first time in your marriage, prayed together through a whole book of the Bible. I trust you are sensing momentum, encouragement, confidence, and joy together!

For more information and resources about praying with your wife, go to www.justsaytheword.net or contact@justsaytheword.net

DISCUSSIONS TO HELP HUSBANDS JOURNEY TOGETHER

Discussion Guide 1— The Husband's Struggle

Review and Discuss:

- Spiritual connectivity for most Christian couples is haphazard and occasional, lacking intentionality and regularity.
- As husbands, we frequently feel as though we are not creative enough nor spiritual enough to regularly lead our wives in prayer, so we hit the "snooze button" on God's alarm clock.
- Allowing the Bible to show us what to pray can provide a fresh and effective path for our prayers.

Conversation:

1. Has the spiritual connectivity between you and your wife been haphazard and occasional? What has caused you to stall?
2. What kinds of things have you been pursuing to enhance spiritual influence in your marriage and home?
3. In what ways do you sense this is God's appointed time for you to stop snoozing and respond to the alarm?
4. What grade would you give yourself concerning spiritual influence and leadership

in your marriage? How do you arrive at this
grade?

Take Action:

Do you owe your wife an apology?

The first step in the *Just Say the Word* journey
is to share with your wife about the revelation God
has given you. Tell her of your new commitment
by God's grace. If an apology is necessary: a true
apology does not only express sorrow but also asks
for forgiveness. However, it is important to realize
that forgiveness fully flows only when repentance
is demonstrated. In other words, repentance lived
out over a reasonable time opens the door to
reconciliation and forgiveness in marriage. Our
wives need to see that our apology has substance.
Behavior changes over time and "puts skin" on your
apology. A wife will likely hold some skepticism in
the corner of her heart, so husbands need to live out
their resolve.

Discussion Guide 2—Calling Men Out

Review and Discuss:

- Most Christian husbands struggle with some
  level of burden that they are not quite cutting
  it with spiritual influence in their marriages.
  This is especially evidenced by a lack of
  praying together with their wives.
- We desire to be spiritual leaders, but we don't
  know exactly what to do.

› Our wives do not need or even want us to
discipline them, but they do want and need us
to walk side-by-side with them in the realities
of life. Praying with your wife through the
Bible is a great way to walk with her.

Conversation:
1. Read 1 Peter 3:7 and see which phrase strikes
   you as the most meaningful for your marriage.
   Why?
2. Apart from praying over meals, praying when
   putting children to bed, or praying at a church
   meeting, how often do you and your wife pray
   together—just the two of you?
3. Even church leaders struggle with consistent
   and intentional prayer in their marriages. Why
   do you think we as Christian husbands
   struggle with spiritual leadership in our
   marriages?
4. The pervasive failure in our spiritual
   leadership has many complicated and
   contributing factors. Each man could tell his
   story. However, many men confess the core of
   our abdication comes from an inner fear that
   says, "I know she knows who I really am!"
   Why does this fear prevent us from stepping
   nearer our wives spiritually? How can we
   overcome this obstacle?

Take Action:
1. *Determine to Initiate.* It is important for
   husbands to take the lead. We cannot wait for
   our wives to initiate. If need be, you can

practice praying the Word yourself to get comfortable with it. Ask God to prepare your wife and to give you the words, resolve, and determination to help you overcome self-consciousness and past failures. God's grace and guidance will equip you step up and step in where you know you need to go!

2. *Determine to be Intentional.* Intentionality is the key. As husbands, we are the guardians of this resolution. Think of it this way: perhaps more intentionally than ever before, we are stepping forward to be the spiritual leaders in our marriages and families. While a great thing such as that will sometimes occur by accident, more often than not, great things become reality because we pursue them on purpose. We cannot grow in spiritual leadership by accident. Our spiritual leadership is fueled by what we *intend* to do.

Discussion Guide 3——It's Just that Simple

Review and Discuss:

- God is calling you to a path of intentional spiritual intimacy between husband and wife.
- Read out loud a small selection of verses with your wife, no more than a paragraph. Proceed slowly. Take turns reading.
- Observe the passage together, and share your thoughts. Warning: this is not a teaching time. You and your wife are seeking key ideas to pray from the Bible.

  ◗ Pray together. You and your wife can each
    participate. Use key words and topics from the
    verses to guide you. Pray over your family.
    Focus on the blessings and concerns of today.

Conversation:
  1. What are the benefits of healthy spiritual
     and emotional intimacy in marriage. For
     men? For women? For your children? For your
     grandchildren?
  2. Practice the *Just Say the Word* model. Use
     Colossians 3:1-3 or James 1:19-21 or another
     passage of your choice:
     ◗ Read the verses.
     ◗ Observe the passage together, and share what
       jumps out at you.
     ◗ Pray using your observations as the guide for
       your prayers.
     ◗ How do you think regularly praying with
       your wife will affect your family?

Take Action:
  1. Decide—perhaps with your wife—on a book
     of the Bible to start praying through together.
     Do either of you have a favorite book? You
     might want to start with that one. If not,
     Philippians, Ephesians, or Psalms are great
     books to use for starters.
  2. Find some private time for praying with your
     wife. Many of you are thinking, "It's impossible
     to find the time!" However, the truth is that
     we make time for what we want to make time
     for. Discover what works for your marriage

and family. For some couples, early morning is good. For others, praying together fits better in the evening or just before bedtime. One of you may be a morning person and the other a night person. Perhaps you can experiment with different options. There are no formulas here. You just have to figure out what best facilitates your praying. You solve difficult problems at work. You can handle this challenge at home. I encourage you to flex toward the time that works best for your wife's level of energy and availability.

Discussion Guide 4—Washing through the Word

Review and Discuss:

▶ As a Christian husband and father, you can make a huge difference if you commit to pray more intentionally and regularly with your wife, using the Bible as your guide.

▶ If a thief were coming into your home tonight to ravage your wife, harm your children, and steal your stuff, you would do something about it! We all know the spiritual thief is at hand and that action is needed, and yet we too often do nothing.

▶ Let's join one another in a prayer journey to step toward increased spiritual health in our marriages. We can weave together three provisions from God into a strong cord: marriage, prayer, and the Bible.

Conversation:

1. How have you loved you wife in a sacrificial way in the past?
2. If your wife were sitting here and we asked her about your new commitment to pray with her, using the Bible as the guide, what would she say?
3. What strategies can we embrace to help one another as men step more intentionally toward being the spiritual leaders in our marriages and homes?

Take Action:

1. Find another brother, or band of brothers, and covenant together to pray with your wives using the Bible as your guide. Holding one another accountable is not legalism; it is a healthy way for Christian brothers to journey together through the difficult realities of life.
2. Share the first names of three other Christian brothers you know who need to hear the *Just Say the Word* model. How can you challenge them to join you?

CROSSROADS

Scripture Prayer Guides...
...Especially for Men

Straight from God's Word, here's real help for the man of today. Faced with choices and changes at every turn, we need biblical guidance to enable us to follow where He leads!

The *Crossroads Prayer Guides* emphasize the contrasts of the old man vs. the new man...old spiritual darkness that has been replaced by new light for living in victory... old human weakness that has given way to amazing spiritual strength...these, plus much, much more.

Each *Crossroads Prayer Guide* is based on the difference that faith in Christ makes—and the truth of the transformed life that enables God's man to make right choices. Each pocket-sized Guide takes you through seven days of Scripture and prayer examples to point to the reality of God's provision for every option you face.

Check them out in greater detail on our website: www.prayerpowerministries.com

Click on Products, then Prayer Guides and then Crossroads. You will find help as you continue seeking God's way as spiritual leader of your wife and family!

Twelve Crossroads titles are now available:

Flee and Pursue   Loss / Gain   Now/Then
Old Man / New Man   Sacrifice / Reward   Young / Old
Darkness / Light   Shadow / Substance   Temporal / Eternal
Weakness / Strength   Empty / Full   Begin / End

www.prayerpowerministries.com

Prayer Power
Helping God's people learn to pray.

P.O. Box 801368 • Dallas, TX 75380-1368 • 800 949 PRAY
email: prayerpower@learntopray.org

More.

THE JUST SAY WORD

a simple way
to increase your
passion for God
and your wife

Sam Ingrassia

Learn More. Find More. Buy More!
www.justsaytheword.net

email: contact@justsaytheword.net